GUITARIST'S GUIDE TO TAB

BY ARTHUR DICK

Wise Publications
London/ New York/ Paris/ Sydney/
Copenhagen/ Madrid/ Tokyo

£4.95

Exclusive Distributors:
Music Sales Limited
8/9 Frith Street,London W1D 3JB, England.
Music Sales Corporation
257 Park Avenue South, New York, NY10010,
United States of America.
Music Sales Pty Limited
120 Rothschild Avenue, Rosebery, NSW 2018, Australia.

Order No. AM969936
ISBN 0-7119-8797-1
This book © Copyright 2001 by Wise Publications

Written and arranged by Arthur Dick
Music processed by Paul Ewers
Cover design by Mike Bell
Book design, layout and editing by Sorcha Armstrong
Printed in the United Kingdom by
Printwise (Haverhill) Limited, Suffolk.

Your Guarantee of Quality
As publishers, we strive to produce every book to the highest
commercial standards.
The music has been freshly engraved and the book has been
carefully designed to minimise awkward page turns and to make
playing from it a real pleasure.

Music Sales' complete catalogue describes thousands of titles and
is available in full colour sections by subject, direct from Music
Sales Limited. Please state your areas of interest and send a
cheque/postal order for £1.50 for postage to: Music Sales Limited,
Newmarket Road, Bury St. Edmunds, Suffolk IP33 3YB.

www.musicsales.com

INTRODUCTION

Wouldn't it be wonderful to transform what you see written on a piece of music on to the guitar fretboard, and make the music come to life by including all the phrases and nuances associated with the piece?

Tablature (TAB) helps you to do this. It is not a replacement for standard musical notation, it is simply a pictorial version of the music displayed on a guitar fretboard!

If you have ever seen TAB notation, you may have wondered what all the numbers and symbols really mean and how they should be interpreted.

But let's start at the beginning!

THE STAVE

The stave is a set of lines and spaces, each representing a pitch, on which music is written.

The music stave is drawn as five lines with a Treble Clef at the beginning of each line. The notes above and below the stave are shown on leger lines. For example, the six open strings of the guitar are notated as follows:

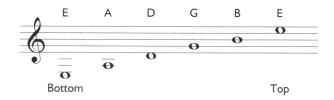

The Guitar

The thickest string is the 6th string. It is shown on the music as the note E, below the stave. It is considered as the bottom string because it is drawn as the bottom line on the TAB diagram. (see below). The next string is A (the 5th string), then D (the 4th string), G (the 3rd string), B (the 2nd string) and E (the 1st or top string).

Throughout this book the right hand is considered the 'pick' or 'strumming' hand, and the left is the 'fret' hand. Pictorially, (sorry if you're left handed – you will have to turn the diagram around!) the guitar neck is viewed from above, as if you are looking down on the fretboard.

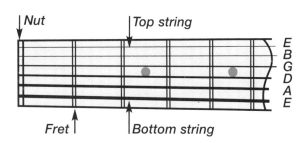

TAB

It is from this pictorial representation that TAB comes about. The TAB 'stave' is a horizontal representation of the six guitar strings viewed from this perspective. The position of the headstock and the nut are not usually shown as part of the TAB stave. This leaves only the six lines representing the six strings of the guitar with the lowest string (low E) as the bottom line and the top string (high E) as the top line.

To tell you which note to play on any given string, a number is placed on the corresponding line of the TAB. Each number refers to a fret position, e.g. F on the third leger line below the stave translates to '1' on the bottom line of the TAB. This means placing your finger on the space on the 6th string between the nut and the 1st fret.

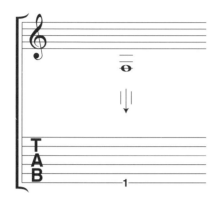

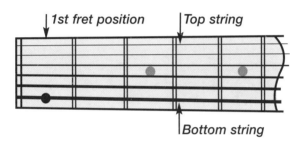

1st fret position   Top string

Bottom string

TAB Stave

The TAB stave is always written directly underneath the music stave. Each number (i.e. fret position) on the TAB corresponds to a musical note vertically above on the music stave.

In the example below, the open strings of the guitar are written on the music stave, and the corresponding TAB equivalents are written directly underneath.

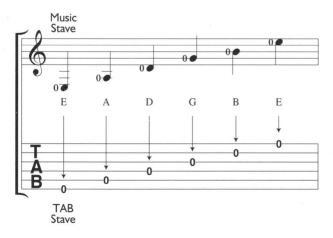

A zero is used to denote an open string on the TAB. (On the music stave a small 0 is sometimes placed to the left of the note to indicate an open string as opposed to the fret equivalent.)

With this method we can designate the string and fret position for any note on the music stave.

When two notes are played together they are displayed vertically on the both staves. Similarly with chords (3 notes or more); what you see on the music stave visually translates to the number on TAB. The following example should help make this clear.

Unfortunately, TAB notation doesn't give us everything we need to produce the perfect performance. Fingering detail (which fingers to use to press the strings down on to the frets) is often missing, and there's no way to show rhythm notation, which gives information about the time values of the notes.

In the previous example, the two bars are best played using the following left-hand fingering. Try alternative fingering to see which is the most suitable if you are unsure. Sometimes fingering is not always obvious or even particularly important. It is up to you and your preferred choice.

The next example shows two fingering patterns for the same phrase (the TAB of course is the same for both).

Musically the note is tied across the bar.

In TAB only the point at which the note is first struck is shown.

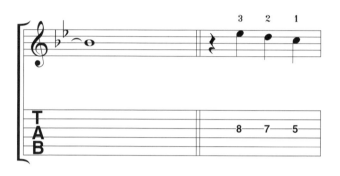

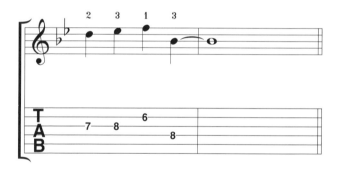

Time Values

The second instruction, the time value of each note, is not directed from TAB. Although the TAB clearly defines the pitch of the note which is to be played on the fretboard, you have to look above to the music stave to understand the precise note value and rhythm of the phrase you are playing. There is no short cut – the TAB gives no time value to any of the notes. This is why you'll rarely see TAB without standard musical notation above it.

It makes sense, then, to be familiar with the most common time-values (if you're not sure, have a look at some theory books – see pages 31-32 for a selection). If you are playing a part that has been transcribed from a recording, then of course you can listen to the musical phrase and its precise rhythm for yourself.

MUSICAL INSTRUCTIONS

There are many musical instructions which can be given to a note or group of notes, some of which are quite specific, and others which are open to interpretation by you. Let's look at some in detail.

Octaves

8va is written above the music stave and indicates that the notes that follow should be played an octave higher than written. 15ma indicates a 2-octave transposition.

8vb is written below the music stave and indicates that the notes that follow should be played an octave lower than written.

loco. cancels all of these instructions.

Have a look at these examples:

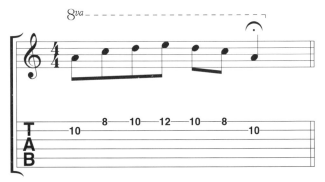

The TAB shows the note positions played up an octave

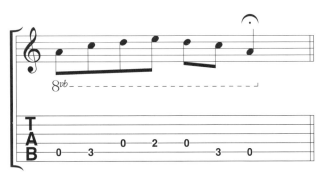

The TAB shows the note positions played down an octave

loco. cancels the 8va instruction, the TAB changes accordingly

Staccato

Staccato (meaning 'detached') shortens the note. It is indicated by a dot over the note on the music stave. To clarify the difference between long and short notes in a phrase, a line is sometimes placed over the long notes.

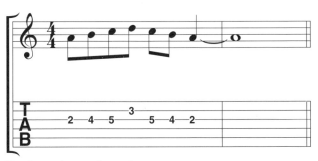

Unaltered note lengths

Staccato – shortened note lengths

Mixture of long and short note lengths

Note: the TAB is the same in both of these examples.

Glissando

The glissando instruction is shown linking two notes with a slur and a line, i.e. sliding down from E to C in the first example or up from D to G in the second. In each case, the first note is struck but the second note sounds without being re-struck.

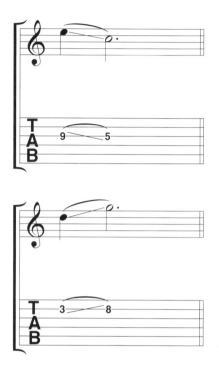

A glissando can also be used to slide a note 'off the fretboard' or used to indicate sliding up to a note from a non-specific point.

See the examples below:

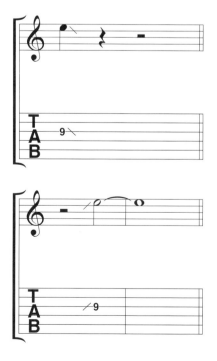

Glissando With Re-Strike

Sometimes the piece of music will indicate that the second note is to be re-struck. In the second example below, the absence of a slur denotes that the second note should be struck.

Compare this with the first example, which is a normal glissando. Remember, a normal glissando will be shown with a slur and a line between the two notes. If the slur isn't present, re-strike the second note.

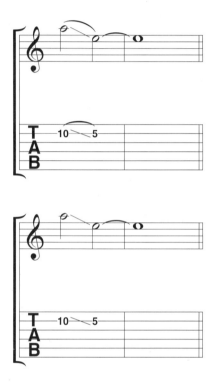

Tremolo

Another musical instruction you might come across is tremolo. This basically means that you should strum or pick the notes up and down as fast as possible, and is indicated by a series of lines through the note tail, and above the TAB.

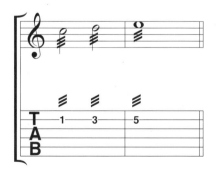

Vibrato

There are two ways to produce vibrato on a note. Vibrato is created by minute variations in pitch, giving the note an expressive quality, and can be done either by the finger, or by using the tremolo arm (or whammy bar).

The precise amount of vibrato is left entirely to the discretion of the performer. The use of vibrato in jazz, blues and rock music is especially noticeable where the effect becomes a characteristic trademark of the performer's style.

Finger Vibrato

This literally means 'shaking' the note with your finger and is indicated on the music and TAB by placing a wavy line over the note.

Compare the following examples.

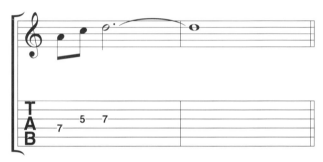

No vibrato

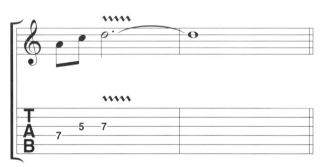

With finger vibrato

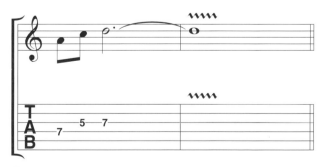

Delayed vibrato

Tremolo Arm Vibrato

By varying the movement of the whammy bar, a vibrato effect can be created. The more the arm is depressed, the greater the depth of vibrato. Again, the amount of expression created by the arm movement is not easy to display on the music and is left to the performer's discretion.

Dive Bombs

The tremolo arm can also be used for other effects. A 'dive bomb' is created by striking the note(s) and simultaneously depressing the arm to drop the pitch to an indefinite point.

The arm can also be used to create bends up to a note, i.e. strike the note with the arm already depressed and then release, bringing the note up to pitch.

The interval of the bend is shown next to the tremolo arm symbol. Each ½ tone is equivalent to a 1 fret interval, so -1½ means the note should be 3 frets lower, and -2½ means it should be 5 frets lower.

Pulling the tremolo arm upwards would be marked with a + symbol.

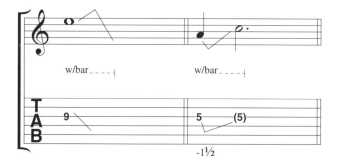

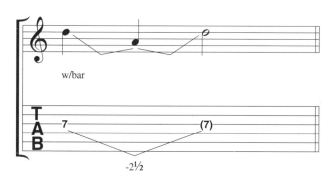

STRING BENDS

This section will deal with all the different types of string bends you are likely to encounter. The most common way of bending a string is up, i.e. across the guitar neck towards you. Bend upwards unless otherwise instructed.

The amount of bending, i.e. the pitch to which the string should be raised, is firstly a musical decision, and secondly, a practical one. How far can a string physically be bent? Obviously, the heavier the string gauge, the greater the tension and the more difficult it becomes to bend a particular string. However, the higher up the neck you play, the closer the frets become and the easier it is to make a bend over a given interval.

In the following examples the 2nd and 3rd strings are used to demonstrate bends from an interval of a semi-tone (½ tone bend, equivalent to one fret) to a major 3rd (2 tone bend, equivalent to 4 frets). The music displays two notes, the first note (called a grace note, and written smaller than normal) is bent up to the second (principal) note of a designated time-value (crotchet, minim, etc).

The TAB also reflects this by using a smaller number for the grace note, indicating that it should be bent up to the main note.

There is no need to anticipate the bend before the beat. The grace note is played on the beat and the bend should occur as quickly as possible. The exact speed is dependent upon the tempo and style of the music as well as the player's 'feel'.

In each case the string in question is bent upwards to the desired pitch.

Quarter-Tone Bend

A quarter-tone bend, also known as a 'decorative' bend, is a common embellishment given to a note which requires the pitch of the note to be fractionally raised by a ¼ tone.

In contrast with the previous bends, the ¼ tone bend does not attempt to establish a definite new pitch.

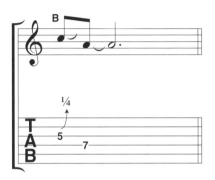

Pre-Bend

This is sometimes referred to as a 'ghost' bend.

Besides bending from one note up to another, the already bent note can be released and allowed to fall back to its original pitch, i.e. the note is bent first and then struck. Where the release of the bend starts and finishes is indicated by the time value of the two notes in question. The rate of the release depends on the tempo of the music as well as the individual's interpretation.

To perform a pre-bend, bend the string as indicated (i.e. a half or full tone), strike the string, and release to the pitch of the second note.

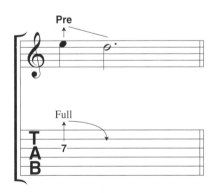

Bend And Hold

In the example that follows, the first note is hit and bent as indicated, i.e. the grace note (G) is played on the beat and immediately bent up to the A (full tone bend) and held for three beats before being released again on to the fourth beat when the G is re-struck.

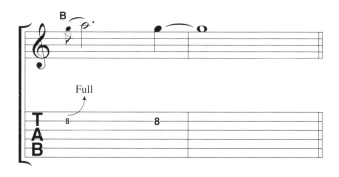

With this example, the first note (G) is bent to the A over a period of one crotchet beat and held for two beats before being released on the fourth beat when the G is played.

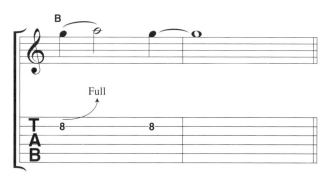

Bend And Release

The bend and release of a note can be combined into a single action by striking the string, bending it as directed and then releasing the bend without striking the string for a second time. As in the previous examples, the speed of the bend (and release) is determined by the time values of the notes in the phrase. The first example demonstrates a grace note bend, so play the bend as quickly as possible.

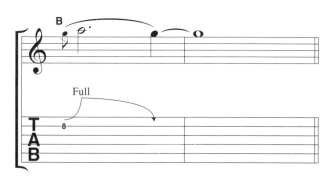

This second example demonstrates a bend from G to A over the period of a crotchet beat, so bend over one beat, hold for two, and then release back to G without re-striking, holding the G for 5 beats.

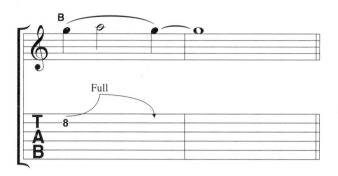

Bend, Hold And Release

This is similar to a bend and release, but uses a slightly different symbol, which is used to denote tied notes. Strike the note and bend up as indicated, hold for the duration of the tied notes (dotted line in the TAB), then release back to the original note without re-striking.

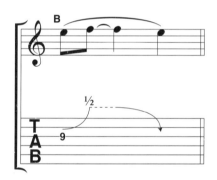

Compound Bend And Release

This idea can be taken further by repeating the process of a bend followed by a release without re-striking the string. Obviously, the string has to sustain over a length of time in order to be able to do this! The vibrato type effect is represented in the following manner.

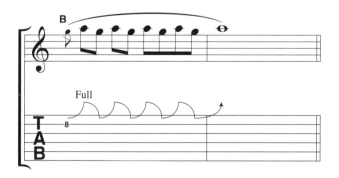

Bend And Re-strike

Until now, a bend has been created by striking the first note and bending accordingly to the desired pitch. To indicate that the second note of the bend should be re-struck (the note being bent to), the symbol ► is placed over the note.

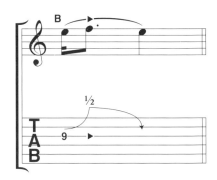

Bend And Multiple Re-strike

As bend and re-strike, but re-strike every time the ► symbol occurs. In this example, bend up a whole tone from C to D and then re-strike six times before releasing (without re-striking C).

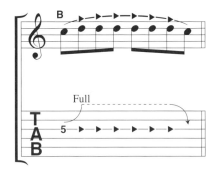

Bend And Tap

This is a fairly rare notation. Bend the note as indicated, and then tap the higher fret while still holding the bend (the tap is indicated by the + symbol). See page 25 for more about tapping.

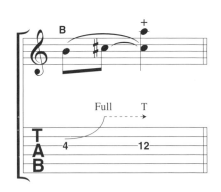

Unison Bend

To create a unison bend, you need to play the same note simultaneously on adjacent strings by bending the lower string up to the pitch of the top one. In this example the note E is struck on the 2nd string (5th fret) while the D at the 7th fret (3rd string) is bent up a tone (to E) so creating a unison note.

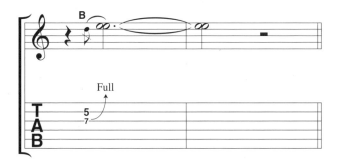

Staggered Unison Bend

Rather than striking both strings simultaneously, the unison bend can be 'staggered', so that the lower note is struck first and bent to the correct pitch. While it is still sounding the higher string is then played. How fast this process occurs is dependent on the time value of each note.

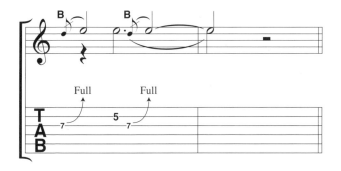

String Bends And Vibrato

String bend notation is generally quite specific, but the rate at which it should happen depends on the piece of music and the player's interpretation.

In a similar way the speed and timing of vibrato is not precisely notated. The sign ⌇⌇⌇⌇ does not indicate the rate and depth of the vibrato effect although its time position can be approximately shown by its placement within the music.

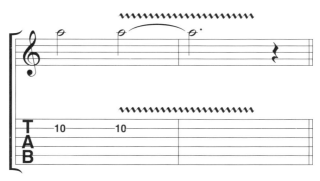

Note with vibrato

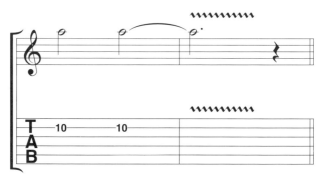

Note with vibrato delayed

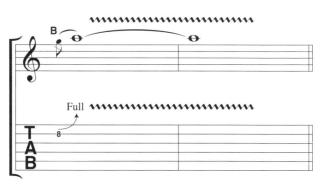

Bent note with vibrato

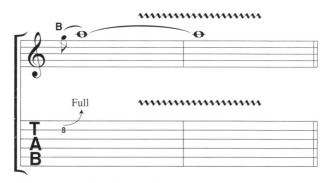

Bent note with vibrato delayed

HAMMER-ONS AND PULL-OFFS

Hammer-Ons

A hammer-on is indicated by a slur between adjacent notes, where the second note is higher than the first.

Rather than striking every note in the phrase, the first note (C) is struck, but the following note (D) is played by hammering the next finger down on the 7th fret without striking the string again.

In terms of the fret hand fingering, the first finger frets C at the 5th fret on the 3rd string and the string is played to sound the C note. To play the following note (D), the third finger hammers down on to the 7th fret of the 3rd string.

Compare the following examples:

Normally

With hammer-ons

Pull-Offs

A pull-off is indicated by a slur between adjacent notes, where the second note is lower than the first.

The process just described for hammer-ons can be applied to a descending phrase, using pull-offs.

The first note (D) is played at the 7th fret on the 3rd string. The third finger which frets the D is then pulled off in such a manner as to pluck the C which is being fretted by the first finger at the 5th fret. This is carried out without re-striking the string.

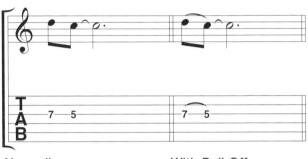

Normally   *With Pull-Off*

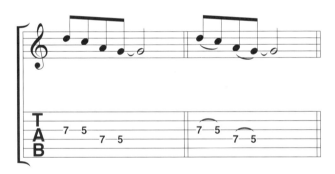

Normally   *With Pull-Off*

Multiple Hammer-Ons And Pull-Offs

Hammer-ons and pull-offs can be applied to a succession of notes in a variety of ways. (Obviously, the notes are all played on the same string!)

After the first note has been struck, the notes that follow may be played by a repetition of hammer-ons (if the notes are going upwards) and pull-offs (if the notes are going downwards).

Have a look at this example, which uses alternating hammer-ons and pull-offs.

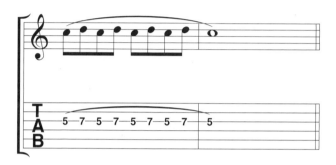

This example uses a mixture of hammer-ons and pull-offs.

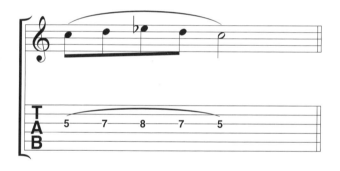

MUSICAL ORNAMENTS

Here's a guide to the most common musical ornaments that you are likely to come across.

Trills

If the hammer-on/pull-off action is performed fast enough, a trill effect is produced. The two notes in this action are notated with a trill mark (*tr*) above them, followed by a wavy line.

If this abbreviation is simply written above a single note it is presumed that the second note of the trill is the next note above in the scale. If this is not the case the two participating notes are written out.

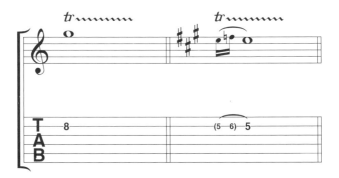

NB: In the key of A, the second note of the trill would normally be F♯, hence the need, in the second example, to show two notes, E and F♮.

Grace Notes

We have already mentioned the grace note, which is played on the beat as quickly as possible.

In the following example, the A will be struck on the beat and quickly pulled-off to play the G.

In a similar fashion the opposite can be performed – the G is played on the beat followed by hammering-on to the A.

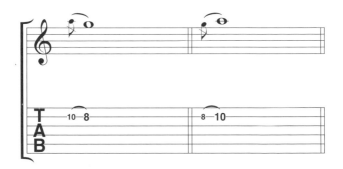

Tapping

Tapping is transcribed using a + symbol and a corresponding T in the TAB above the note to be tapped. This note is played by the right hand, by striking the string with the side of the plectrum (or finger) over the fret indicated.

In the example below, the G is sounded by striking the 3rd string at the 12th fret using the side of the plectrum, or finger of the pick hand.

The next note (B) is then sounded by a pull-off action between the 12th fret (covered by the pick hand) an the 4th fret (fretted by the first finger, fret hand). The note (C) that follows is played by hammering the second finger down on the 5th fret.

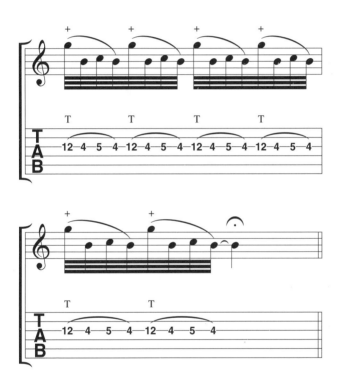

Rake

Raking across the strings is a perfect description as the plectrum (or finger) is literally raked, or dragged, across the strings. The effect is of a controlled strum upwards (or downwards) across the strings, creating a fast arpeggio.

The resonance of the strings can be regulated by the palm of the pick hand partially covering the strings as they are played. This damping or palm mute produces a staccato effect. The more the strings are damped, the shorter the notes become.

The strings can be totally muted by a combination of the right hand partially covering the strings and the frethand covering the fret(s), but not actually pressing the string down. This produces a non-pitched percussive sound.

Here are some examples:

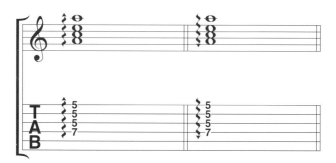

Rake Up   *Rake Down*

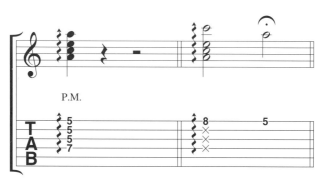

Rake up – strings   *Rake up – strings*
partially damped   *muted except top note*

Harmonics

Natural harmonics occur on the open strings at certain points along the length of the string (commonly the 5th, 7th and 12th frets). Here's how to do it: gently place, without pressing down, the finger of your fretting hand on to the string right over the metal fret, not in between (as if sounding a normal note).

Strike the string with your pick hand, and you should hear a resonant, ghostly sound, higher in pitch than the actual note at that fret.

Here are some examples at the 12th fret. Remember, don't press down the string – simply place your finger gently on to the string above the fret wire.

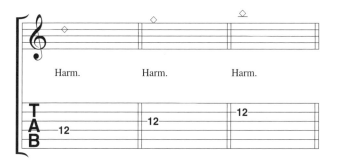

Here are some examples at the 7th fret. The harmonics created at this position sound an octave higher than the fretted note.

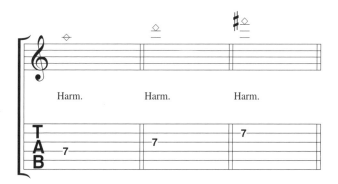

Artificial Harmonics

Artificial harmonics are created from a stopped, or fretted, string. The harmonic is played by picking and plucking the string in a kind of pinching action, an octave (12 frets) above the note that is being fretted.

In the example below, the large number on the TAB refers to where your fretting hand should be placed. The smaller number in brackets indicates the fret number at which you should place your strumming hand on the string (not pressing down!).

You now need to pluck the string, also with your strumming hand. Tricky!

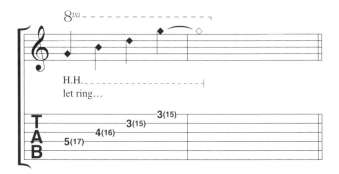

Other Musical Ornaments

There are other, less widely used, ornaments (mordent, turn, appoggiatura and others) which are usually performed using the hammer-on or pull-off - but these are generally not found in most modern music scores and especially TAB.

If you would like more information on these, please refer to one of the music theory books available from the Music Sales catalogue (see pages 31-32 for more details).

CONCLUSION

Notation using standard musical text and TAB gives you a more complete musical picture, but the entire performance can never be precisely written down. The expression and feel can only be partially conveyed on paper.

You have to listen to the original recording of the transcription and relate what you see to what you hear or interpret the written directions as you feel fit. Experience will help – the more you play the better you will get.

However, one Italian direction that is unambiguous is the term *fine*, it means 'the end'!

ADDITIONAL MUSICAL INSTRUCTIONS

There are many musical instructions that can accompany a piece of music. Many of them are Italian words indicating expression as well as general directions to the performer. You can find out more about these in a good theory book.

(♪)	ghost note; a very quiet or nearly silent note
>	accent; this symbol appears above notes which should be accented
V	Roman numerals (most commonly used in classical guitar notation) indicate the position of the fret hand index finger.
CV	full barre; Roman numerals indicate correct fret
½CV	half barre; Roman numerals indicate correct fret
♪ = 72	tempo is instructed as 72 crotchet beats per minute
ad lib.	the speed and interpretation is left to the discretion of the performer
rit.	abbreviation for ritenuto, meaning hold back
rall.	abbreviation for rallentando, meaning slow down
poco a poco	little by little, or gradually; e.g. poco a poco cresc. means gradually get louder
◁	getting gradually louder
▷	getting gradually softer
N.C.	No Chord

Fretboard fingering indicated by:	T = thumb 1 = index finger 2 = middle finger 3 = ring finger 4 = little finger
Pick hand fingering indicated by:	P = thumb 1 = index finger M= middle finger A = ring finger

FURTHER READING

If you've enjoyed this book, why not check out some of the other great titles suitable for your guitar case, available from all good music and book shops, or in case of difficulty, directly from Music Sales (see p2) or **www.musicroom.com**

Guitar Case Chord Book
AM35841
Our best-selling small format chord book, with clear, readable diagrams and no page flipping. A handy sized reference book to all the most essential chords.

Guitar Case Scale Book
AM76217
A concise thesaurus of essential and practical forms for study and practice. Tips on using scales to build speed, endurance and fretboard fluency.

Start Reading Music
AM80219
A proven, step-by-step method on mastering the basics of sight reading – whether you are an instrumentalist, singer or composer, this book tells you all you need to know.

300 Tips And Tricks For Guitar
AM945220
A practical guide for every guitarist. Includes choosing an instrument, reading music, chords and scales, blues, rock, jazz, country and funk riffs, and much more.

Gig Bag Book Of Scales For All Guitarists
AM941370
Contains over 180 scales in twelve keys, with fingering suggestions and five different scale positions.

FURTHER READING (cont.)

Gig Bag Book Of Guitar TAB Chords
AM943250
Over 2,100 chords for all guitarists, compiled by Mark Bridges and presented in unique guitar TAB format. Each diagram illustrates the fingering, inversion and notes of every chord.

Gig Bag Book Of Arpeggios For All Guitarists
AM946902
The ultimate arpeggio reference book for all guitarists, containing 240 arpeggios in all 12 keys. The handy fretboard diagrams illustrate the finger positions.

Tuning Your Guitar
AM35858
Easy-to-follow text and diagrams: will do wonders even for the so-called 'tone deaf'!

How To Use A Capo For Guitar
HLE00695255
Play with a capo in the style of The Beatles, Keith Richards, The Byrds and many more. An essential reference for all guitarists.

The Little Book Of Music Theory
AM954855
Introduction to the basics of music theory – accidentals, rhythm and time, major and minor keys, intervals, modes, scales, and chords, in one handy little book!

5/01 (40284